BEST-KEPT SECRETS OF

PRAGUE

Publisher and Creative Director: Nick Wells
Commissioning Editor: Polly Prior
Project Editor: Josie Mitchell
Art Director: Mike Spender
Layout Design: Jane Ashley
Copy Editor: Ramona Lamport
Proofreader: Amanda Crook
Indexer: Helen Snaith

FLAME TREE PUBLISHING
6 Melbray Mews
London SW6 3NS
United Kingdom

www.flametreepublishing.com

First published 2018

18 20 22 21 19
1 3 5 7 9 10 8 6 4 2

A CIP record for this book is available from the British Library upon request.

Courtesy of **Shutterstock.com** and © the following contributors: 12 Premysl; 13 badahos; 14, 147 PHB.cz (Richard Semik); 15 Ralf Siemieniec; 16 Andrew Mayovskyy; 17 Alex van Eekelen; 18 VarnakovR; 20 Peter Zurek; 21 Delpixel; 22 DaLiu; 24 dimbar76; 25, 40, 62, 92, 96 frantic00; 26 Yasonya; 28, 130 RossHelen; 29 Kiev.Victor; 31 Premysl; 33 Jason Batterham; 34 Lyd Photography; 36 Radiokafka; 37 Ignus Kruklitis; 38 PeterVrabel; 42, 45, 54 4kclips; 44 Grachev Alexey; 46, 117 maziarz; 47 SergeyPhoto7; 48 FrBohac; 50, 76, 106, 107, 149 Josef Hanus; 51 Dominik Michalek; 52 YRABOTA; 53, 102 josefkubes; 55, 103 Angelina Dimitrova; 58, 180 Nadezda Murmakova; 59 pryzmat; 64 WhiteHaven; 65 M-SUR; 68 Gabriel Georgescu; 70, 122 Kajano; 72 DeepGreen; 73 hydra viridis; 74 Tanya Kramer; 77, 118, 120, 144 Capture Light; 78 Catarina Belova; 80 photoiconix; 81 Deyan Denchev; 83 smereka; 85 DashaR; 86 agean; 88 Sofron; 89 Marben; 90, 112, 186, 187 kaprik; 93 Ireine; 98 Lipskiy; 100 Zdenka Simekova; 104, 151 Sergey Kohl; 110 yakub88; 114 Red-feniks; 116 emka74; 119 O_Voltz; 123 Khromova Anna; 124 Grisha Bruev; 125 Layue; 126, 170 Tuomas Lehtinen; 128, 141 PHOTOCREO Michal Bednarek; 129 Ozgur Guvenc; 133 Mariia Golovianko; 134 Will Howe; 136 Sanchai Kumar; 138 Papuchalka – kaelaimages; 139 bango; 140 Maciej Bledowski; 142 Alla Koval; 143 Anibal Trejo; 146 arazu; 148 Michal Zduniak; 150 InnaFelker; 154 Uhryn Larysa; 155, 165, 174 islavicek; 156 trabantos; 157 Rus S; 158 Vladimir Muller; 160 Taborsky; 162 yykkaa; 164 Jiri Vaclavek; 166 Shiler; 167 Lost Mountain Studio; 168 Estea; 171 Vladimir Sazonov; 172 2xSamara.com; 173 Joymsk140; 175 Nenad Basic; 177 czech wanderer; 178 Forance; 179 Anrephoto; 182 ZM_Photo; 183 Afflamen; 184 Aivita Arika; 188 Jule_Berlin. Courtesy of **SuperStock.com** and © the following contributors: 30, 41 Peter Erik Forsberg/age footstock; 57 Christian Goupi/age footstock; 84, 99 Peter Erik Forsberg/age footstock; 115, 132 Radim Beznoska/age footstock; 161 Birgitte Mejer/age footstock. Courtesy of **Getty Images** and © the following contributors: 39 Lonely Planet; 56, 94, 176 Richard Nebesky; 66 Image Source; 69 Graham Monro/gm photographics; 82 Meißner/ullstein bild; 111 Tuomas Lehtinen; 137 Peter Zelei images. Courtesy of and **© Jewish Museum, Prague**: 32.

ISBN 978-1-78664-789-4

Printed in China | Created, Developed & Produced in the United Kingdom

BEST-KEPT SECRETS OF

PRAGUE

MICHAEL ROBINSON

FLAME TREE
PUBLISHING

CONTENTS

INTRODUCTION

According to the official World Travel Market figures for 2016, Prague is the fifth most visited city in Europe, outperforming Barcelona, Vienna and Amsterdam. When one considers that the city only emerged from over 50 years of occupation by oppressive regimes – of Nazism and then Communism – in 1990, this is an impressive statistic and Prague may even rival the tourist giants, London and Paris, in the next decade for visitor numbers. So what are Prague's attractions? The two giants of tourism both have their iconic and recognizable motifs – Big Ben in London and the Eiffel Tower in Paris – but Prague is able to match them with its majestic medieval Charles Bridge (*see* page 22), which symbolizes its historical heritage and is probably the most photographed site in the city, its bustling activity of street sellers, sketch artists and musicians there to provide a fuller gamut of culture beyond its history. This book then is not just a historical biography of the city but one that takes you on a journey interweaving actual history with mythology, and folklore with modern traditions.

The city of Prague consists of five ancient towns that developed around the Vltava River. They are Hradčany, the oldest part that contains the castle and St Vitus Cathedral (*see* page 136), and Lesser Town (Malá Strana), both of which are situated to the west of the river. On the east side are the districts of Josefov (formerly the Jewish Quarter), Old Town (Staré Město) and New Town (Nové Město). All five districts were established by the fourteenth century. By the 1920s the outlying districts, such as Vinohrady, had also been included into Greater Prague, a city that today has in excess of two million inhabitants.

Prague's roots as the ancient capital of the Kingdom of Bohemia were laid down in the tenth century when two citadels were established, one at Vyšehrad on the east bank of the river just south of New Town, and Hrad any. Two members of the Přemyslid dynasty, who were constantly feuding for control, established the two opposing castles. In 935 one of the ruling princes, Wenceslas, was murdered by his bother Boleslav. The pious Wenceslas, who was eventually canonized, became the patron saint of Bohemia.

It was, however, in the fourteenth century that Prague became significantly more important following the coronation of the King of Bohemia, Charles IV (1316–78) in 1346. When he became Holy Roman Emperor in 1355, the imperial court was moved to Prague, and Charles was successful in establishing some of the constitutional structures of the empire, which held sway until the nineteenth century. The period of his reign is often referred to as the 'Golden Age' of Prague, since Charles was also responsible for building the new 'Stone Bridge', later renamed in his honour to replace the Judith Bridge damaged by flooding, which for the next 300 years was the only means of crossing the river. Charles also commissioned the building of St Vitus Cathedral and founded the University of Prague, the first of its kind in Central Europe.

It was the first Czech rector of the university, Jan Hus (1369–1415), who radically changed the course of Prague's history in the next century, promulgating a Reformation that predated Luther by about a century. Hus deplored certain practices of the Catholic Church – such as indulgences – but his continuous sermonizing eventually led to his execution for heresy and the beginning of the so-called Hussite Wars, a series of crusades under the aegis of the Pope against Hus's followers, that lasted until 1434. It was the less radical arm of the Bohemian Reformation, the Ultraquists, who finally brokered a peace with the Catholics, the subsequent Bohemian kings being tolerant of both practices. This tenuous and difficult hold on power continued after 1526 when Ferdinand I (1503–64) became king, and later, in 1558, Holy Roman Emperor. Ferdinand was the first of the Austrian Habsburg dynasty to rule Bohemia, a situation that lasted until 1918.

His grandson Rudolph II (1552–1612) was, however, less effectual as a leader and politician, his reign contributing to the Battle of White Mountain in 1620 that would see the return of Catholic primacy in Prague for the next 300 years. Besides moving the capital of the Habsburg Empire from Vienna to Prague, Rudolph II was also a great patron of the arts, acquiring a large collection of Italian Renaissance paintings. Furthermore, he enlarged Prague Castle (*see* page 134) to house the collection. His interest in the occult and alchemy were legendary and gave the city its mystical reputation, one it still enjoys today.

Despite the best efforts of Rudolph II and his predecessors, tolerance of all faiths in Prague came to an abrupt end when Ferdinand II (1578–1637), an avowed Catholic, became King of Bohemia and Holy Roman Emperor. Protestant revolts took place, leading to the Thirty Years War between 1618 and 1648, in which eight million people died. Other countries were also involved, with England, Sweden and Holland supporting the Protestants, and France and Spain siding with the Catholics.

Prague at this time became a centre of artistic excellence, as the Catholic Counter-Reformation was in full swing. The Papal Council of Trent, completed in 1563, specifically encouraged the use of the flamboyant Baroque style in art and architecture, designed to show and reaffirm Catholic supremacy. An example of this flamboyance is the Santa Casa Chapel at the Loreto in Hradčany (*see* page 146), significantly designed by the Italian architect Giovanni Orsi (1600–41), and begun in 1626. The Loreto was built as a sanctuary, a site of pilgrimage, based on the one in the small Italian town of the same name. Within the Loreto is also the Church of the Nativity, a magnificently ornate building, its interior an exemplar of Baroque mastery. The tower has a carillon of 27 bells that peal 'A Thousand Times we Praise Thee' every hour during the daytime, to honour the Virgin Mary.

A new period of arts patronage continued in the late eighteenth century with the coronation of Josef II (1741–90), often referred to as the 'Music King'. He commissioned the building of the Estates Theatre (*see* page 12), which on completion in 1783 held the premiere of three operas by Wolfgang Amadeus Mozart (1756–91), including *Don Giovanni* in 1787. The theatre is the only extant of its type in which the great composer performed. The new flowering of artistic endeavour followed a period of disaster in Prague, firstly with the Great Fire in 1689 and then an outbreak of plague that claimed the lives of at least 12,000 inhabitants. In 1744 Prague was attacked by Prussian forces who destroyed about a quarter of the city, including large parts of St Vitus Cathedral (*see* page 136). Nevertheless, the city soon regained prestige, as it became a centre for wealthy merchants and nobles. Josef II was also responsible for a new administration in the city that saw four of the five districts amalgamated into a city-state. The Old Jewish Quarter was omitted, but renamed Josefov, with its inhabitants allowed more freedoms than before. Since the medieval period, Jews were forced to live within the ghetto, and at different times during Prague's history were subjected to pogroms and the wearing of distinctive clothing.

Josef II's nephew was Francis II (1768–1835), the last of the Holy Roman Emperors, forced to renounce the title in the face of Napoleonic aggression. Instead he became the first of the newly styled Emperors of Austria, a title assumed by his son Ferdinand I (1793–1875), who was also the last crowned King of Bohemia as Ferdinand V. The seat of the Emperor of Austria became Vienna, with Prague and Bohemia becoming part of its empire. The longest reigning ruler of Bohemia was Franz Josef I (1830–1916), although he was never crowned king, preferring instead the title Emperor of Austria, which he inherited in 1848. One of his first acts was to include Josefov within the city of Prague in 1850. During his reign, Franz Josef I was dogged by the Czech National Revival in response to his indifference to Czech nationals. When he came to power in 1848 there was a majority of German speakers in Prague, but by 1880 this had dropped to 14 per cent. Matters were exacerbated in 1882 when Prague University was divided into Czech and German language institutions.

The situation was not resolved until the end of the First World War, the death of the Emperor, the collapse of the empire and the establishment of a free and independent Czechoslovakia with Prague as its capital. Its first president was Tomáš Masaryk (1850–1937) who chose Prague Castle as his seat of government, being re-elected three times and known as the 'Czech Liberator'. He died before seeing his fledgling country occupied by the Nazis in 1939. At the end of the Second World War, Czechoslovakia was occupied again, this time by the Soviets, and was again liberated during the relatively peaceful Velvet Revolution at the end of the Soviet era. In 1990 the country was divided geographically between the Czech Republic with Prague as its capital, and Slovakia whose capital is Bratislava.

Despite these occupations, very few of the old buildings suffered any lasting damage so that today we see a modern city with an efficient transport system, and yet one that has lost

ABSINTHERIE
ABSINTH MUSEUM
HOT WINE
HAVELSKÉ TRŽIŠTĚ
DALÍ
SAUDEK
exhibition
WARHOL
RESTAURANT

OLD TOWN AND JOSEFOV

Despite not being the oldest part of the city, the Old Town is nevertheless the heart of Prague. It is where the Old Town Hall with its famous astronomical clock (*see* page 18) is situated, together with the beautiful twin-towered Church of Our Lady before Týn (*see* page 14). The church overlooks the Old Town Square (*see* page 16), the focal point of the area. Its pastel-coloured buildings on the south and east sides, many of which date from medieval times, provide an ideal location for leisurely strolling, as well as eating and drinking in its many cafés and bars.

To the north of the Old Town is Josefov, an area that since the Middle Ages has seen more than its fair share of persecution and oppression of Jews by Christians. It was not until the middle of the nineteenth century that the area was incorporated into the city itself, having previously been a ghetto. The earlier pogroms and discrimination had desisted when Josef II came to the throne and this area is now also known as Josefov. Many of the old buildings were destroyed in the late nineteenth century for health and sanitation reasons, but several have survived, including the Old New Synagogue, as well as the Old Jewish Cemetery.

PATRIAE ET MUSIS

ESTATES THEATRE

Ovocný Trh, Old Town

The Estates Theatre was built between 1781 and 1783 and financed by Count Nostitz, a member of a noble family from Prague. It is renowned especially for its continuous association with Mozart's operas, since it was at this theatre that two of them were premiered: *Don Giovanni* in 1787 and *Clemenza di Tito* in 1791, the latter on the day of King Leopold's coronation. It is the only theatre still in existence in which Mozart himself performed. Some of the scenes for the film *Amadeus* were shot at the theatre in 1984.

ČECHŮV BRIDGE

Vltava River, Old Town

This lovely Art Nouveau bridge was constructed between 1905 and 1908 and is the shortest of the Prague bridges, linking Josefov with Letná Park, in the Holešovice district (*see* page 154). It was named after the Czech writer Svatopluk Čech (1846–1908), whose novels about 'The Excursions of Mr Brouček' were made into an opera by his fellow countryman Leoš Janáček (1854–1928). On the piers of the bridge overhanging the river on one side are two figures holding torches, symbolic of lighting the path along the river, while on the other are two six-headed hydra figures.

CHURCH OF OUR LADY BEFORE TÝN

Old Town Square, Old Town

One of several striking buildings, as seen here above Old Town Square, its twin towers are visible from many other parts of the city. The church dates from the fourteenth century and is associated with the reform movement of the Hussites, a group of Catholic reformers who existed for about 100 years between the early fifteenth and sixteenth centuries. At the top of the façade between the towers is now a golden statue of the Madonna, which replaced the Hussite 'Ultraquist' symbol of a chalice when the building returned to being a strictly Catholic church in 1619.

RUDOLFINUM

Alšovo Nábřeží, Old Town

Demonstrating the eclecticism of Prague's architecture, this Neoclassical theatre was built between 1876 and 1884, and named in honour of Crown Prince Rudolph of Austria, who officially opened the building. It comprises the Dvořák Hall – one of the oldest, and arguably one of the finest, surviving concert halls in Europe – and is currently the home of the Czech Philharmonic Orchestra, which has been in residence since 1946. It also includes the Gallerie Rudolfinum that houses modern art and is often used for the annual Prague Spring Music festival.

OLD TOWN SQUARE

Old Town

This view of the Old Town Square is looking east towards the Church of Our Lady before Týn (*see* page 14). In the left foreground is the famous Astronomical Clock of the Town Hall. On the south side of the square are pastel-coloured houses with unusual names, such as 'At the Golden Unicorn' and 'At the Blue Star', denoting a figure or symbol that appears on the façade from medieval times when houses were not numbered. Restaurants and cafés mainly occupy the arcades beneath the houses.

OLD TOWN HALL ASTRONOMICAL CLOCK

Old Town Square, Old Town

Dating from 1410, this famous landmark of Prague is truly unique and always gathers a crowd to view the display on the hour, when the figure of Death on the left of the clock (seen in this picture on the right) pulls a rope in his right hand while inverting an hourglass in his left. The rope opens two windows above the dial to reveal a revolving procession of the twelve apostles, led by St Peter. At the end of the procession the clock strikes the hour.

MUNICIPAL HOUSE

Republic Square, Old Town

An Art Nouveau masterpiece, this building stands on the site of the former Royal Court Palace, which was demolished in 1900 to facilitate this new cultural centre. On the façade is a semi-circular mosaic entitled 'Homage to Prague' by the Czech artist Karel Špillar (1871–1939). Above the arched windows are bas-reliefs depicting allegorical figures that symbolize art, science and industry. Many other Czech artists, including Alphonse Mucha (1860–1939), lavishly decorated the interiors with murals, stained glass and sculpture. The centrepiece of the complex is the Smetana Hall, the leading concert venue in Prague.

ZDAR TOBĚ PRAHO
JAK ODOLALAS VĚKY BOUŘÍM

MILUJTE SE · PRAVDY KAŽDEMU

JAN HUS STATUE

Old Town Square, Old Town

In 1915 this very large statue was unveiled to mark the 500th anniversary of Jan Hus's execution as a heretic. He was condemned to die by the Catholic authorities in Prague because of his church reformist proselytizing. Hus pre-dated Luther's Protestant reforms by about a century and was, along with John Wycliffe (1330–84), an early reformer of Catholic doctrine. Hus's execution led to the so-called Hussite Wars that lasted until 1434, when the moderate Ultraquist faction, supported by the Catholics, defeated the more radical Toborite Hussites.

POWDER TOWER

Republic Square, Old Town

Originally one of the eleventh-century gateways into the Old Town, the present tower dates from 1475, intended as an ornamental entrance to the Royal Court building and known originally as the 'New Tower'. The project was, however, abandoned after eight years when King Vladislav II (1456–1516) was forced to flee the city because of pro-Catholic riots. On his return in 1485 he sought the safer sanctuary of the castle where he and his successors held court. Kings never re-used the Royal Court and the Powder Tower was used instead as a gunpowder store, hence its name.

CHARLES BRIDGE

Vltava River, Old Town

One of the most famous in the world, the Charles Bridge is named after King Charles IV, and links the Lesser Town with the Old Town. It is dominated by the Old Town Bridge Tower which has the numerical palindrome 135797531 carved into

its wall, referring to the date and time of the laying of its foundation stone, 9 July 1357 at 5.31 a.m. Charles was a student of astronomy, astrology and the occult, and would have held great store by the symbolic meaning of these dates and figures.

STATUE OF FRANZ KAFKA

Vězeňská, Old Town

This is a surrealist statue of the writer Franz Kafka (1883–1924) that reflects the absurdity and illogical nature of his work. It was made by Jaroslav Róna (b. 1957), and erected in 2003 to commemorate one of Prague's most revered residents. The depiction is of Kafka sitting, as a child would, on the shoulders of a larger figure. The figure is, however, missing and represented by an empty male suit. An interpretation of the empty suit may well be related to Kafka's own alienated relationship with his father, who he regarded as an emotional bully.

ST SALVATOR'S CHURCH

Clementinum, Old Town

Framed by the Gothic arch of the Old Town Bridge Tower, the Baroque façade of St Salvator's Church makes an interesting comparison. The construction of the church began in 1572, with the Baroque features added in the mid-seventeenth century. The church, with its two organs, is used as a concert venue as well as for the usual masses, and forms part of the Clementinum, a large complex of buildings established by the Jesuits for the purpose of higher education, as promoted by the King of Bohemia and Holy Roman Emperor, Rudolph II.

VLTAVA RIVER AND OLD TOWN SKYLINE

Old Town

The Vltava River is the longest in the Czech Republic, and meanders through Prague with 18 bridges erected in the city to traverse its course. The view here is taken from the Lesser Town towards the Old Town, with the Charles Bridge in the right foreground. The large green dome is the Church of St Francis (*see* page 29), and behind that to the left is the Observation Tower of the Clementinum (*see* page 118). In the distance is the 216-m (709-ft) tall Žižkov Television Tower (*see* page 98), and on the far left of the picture in the mid-distance is the Church of Our Lady before Týn (*see* page 14).

SCULPTURE OF THE MAN HANGING OUT

Husova, Old Town

Suspended high above the narrow Husova Street is the sculpture known as *Man Hanging Out* by the controversial Czech artist David Černý (b. 1967). From street level it is a very lifelike depiction of a man hanging on to a flagpole with one hand and has caused some observers to call the emergency services. The figure is, in fact, a sculptural likeness of the psychoanalyst Sigmund Freud, whose ideas about phobias and *Thanatos* (death drive) are reflected here. Černý's own postmodern views question the currency of intellectualism in the twenty-first century.

CHURCH OF ST FRANCIS OF ASSISI

Knight of the Cross Square, Old Town

In 1648, the old thirteenth-century church of the same name was largely destroyed during the Siege of Prague. The present church was erected on the site, its lavish Baroque style being a symbol of Catholic triumphalism as part of Europe's Counter-Reformation. Most spectacular is the painted mural inside the cupola, as shown in this picture. Adjacent to the church is the monastery of the Knights of the Cross with a Red Star, a crusading order founded in the thirteenth century similar to the Knights Hospitaller.

SIGNVM

HAVELSKÉ TRŽIŠTĚ
založeno 1232
ELSKÉ TRŽIŠTĚ

HAVELSKÝ MARKET

Havelská, Old Town

There has been a market on this site since 1232 selling fruit, vegetables and flowers. The tradition is still upheld today, together with handmade crafted goods such as wooden toys. Contemporary to the establishment of the market was the building of the Church of St Gall, seen here in the background. The church, originally one of only four in Prague at the time, was given a Baroque makeover between 1723 and 1738, and its treasures include *Calvary* by the Czech sculptor Ferdinand Brokoff (1688–1731), who was responsible for many of the statues on Charles Bridge.

HOUSE AT THE STONE BELL

Old Town Square, Old Town

On the eastern side of the Old Town Square stands the fourteenth-century burgher house, which had remained hidden from view since 1685 by Baroque remodelling. It was extensively restored to its Gothic origins in the late twentieth century. The restoration has revealed a number of fine Gothic murals on the ceilings and walls, and it has been suggested that the Holy Roman Emperor Charles IV lived here while Prague Castle was being repaired following a fire. The bell attached to the building's corner is alleged to have come originally from the Church of Our Lady before Týn (*see* page 14).

KLAUSEN SYNAGOGUE

U Starého Hřbitova, Josefov

All the synagogues and the Jewish Town Hall in the Quarter are now part of a collective known as the Jewish Museum. Each has a separate story to tell about Jewish life in Prague – and more generally in Bohemia – from the time of the first settlement in the tenth century, detailing the various pogroms and persecutions suffered by the Jews across the ages. Also included in the Jewish Museum is the now reduced Old Jewish Cemetery. The Klausen was built in the seventeenth century and is the only surviving Baroque-style synagogue in Prague.

TOYS AND PUPPETS SHOP

Celetná, Old Town

One of the most enchanting cultural features of Prague is marionettes and puppet theatre. It began in the seventeenth century and became a mainstay in Bohemian theatre and performance. For many less advantaged citizens it was the only form of theatre accessible to them. The most famous puppeteer was Matěj Kopecký (1775–1847) whose descendants continued to make and perform with marionettes into the twentieth century. Today there are several shops in Prague like this one *(Hračky u Zlatého Iva)* selling puppets and it is still possible to see performances at the National Marionette Theatre in Old Town.

CHURCH OF ST SIMON AND ST JUDE

U Milosrdných, Old Town

This rather unusual church, which combines both Gothic and Baroque features, has had something of a chequered history since its first incarnation in the fourteenth century. Originally a Catholic chapel adjoining a hospital, it was acquired and enlarged by the Bohemian Brethren, a Hussite group who occupied it for only five years before it was restored to the Jesuits following the Battle of White Mountain in 1620. The church was deconsecrated in 1950, during the period of Communism, and following the Velvet Revolution has been used as a concert venue for the Prague Symphony Orchestra.

JOSEF KRANNER'S FOUNTAIN

Smetana Embankment, Old Town

Facing the river is the monumental fountain by architect Josef Kranner (1801–71) dedicated to the Holy Roman Emperor Francis I (1708–65), who was married in 1736 to the last of the Habsburg monarchs Marie Theresa (1717–80), and is seen in the centre of the fountain on horseback. The sculpture is by the Czech artist Josef Max (1804–55). The fountain is also known as the Hold of Bohemian Estates and the other allegorical figures, also by Max, symbolize peace, opulence, science, art, industry and commerce, mining and ploughing.

APPLE MUSEUM

Husova, Old Town

Prague has a plethora of unusual small museums, particularly in the Old Town, including this one dedicated to a history of Apple Computers and its founders Steve Jobs (1955–2011) and Steve Wozniak (b. 1950). The story is told through anecdote and a marvellous display of the earliest designs right through to those of the present day. Among the exhibits is the first mass-produced Apple II made in 1979 and the extraordinary first 'portable' Apple Computer made in 1989 that was the size of a large briefcase! There are also displays of the early keyboards and mice.

MUSEUM OF CZECH CUBISM

Celetná, Old Town

The House of the Black Madonna (pictured here) is by the Czech architect Josef Gočár (1880–1945). Inspired by the Cubist style painting and sculpture, he and a group of like-minded designers created a range of buildings, furniture and interiors in Prague. This one was built as a department store in 1911–12, and is today the Museum of Czech Cubism. On the first floor is the Grand Orient Café, which today has a unique Cubist interior informed by its previous incarnation under its original name.

BEDŘICH SMETANA MUSEUM

Old Town

Overlooking the Vltava River is a Renaissance-inspired building that used to be a waterworks for the city. It was re-opened in 1936 as a museum to commemorate the life and works of the father of Czech music, Bedřich Smetana (1824–84). His best known composition is *Má vlast* (My Homeland), a series of symphonic poems written between 1874 and 1879 at a time when the Czech nation was seeking its own identity outside the Austro-Hungarian Empire. The second of the poems is called *Vltava*, but is more often referred to by its Germanic name *Die Moldau*.

PO
PO
OBNOVENO 1925

GUSTAVE FLAUBERT PANÍ BOVARYOVÁ
Kinnan Marjorie Rawlingsová Dieťa divočiny
Pražské povstání 1945
NĚMČINA
J. Starý / Mikropočítač a jeho programování
A hořel snad i kámen
jazveci
MARGITA FIGULI BABYLON
IVAN HUDEC
HĽADANIE POSLEDNÉHO RAJA
FRANCOUZŠTINA PRO S
JAPONCI jak je neznám
Gabriele Wohmannová
DOLF KUNZEL Lidský organismus ve zdraví a nemoci
DOBRODRUŽSTVÍ
KAREL MAY KAPITÁN KAIMAN
EXPLÓZIA
pro RT-aplikace
Hrozné carevny
CHIRS RYAN / VYDRŽ
MURDOCH - AN UNOFFICIAL ROSE
TANEČNÍ LISTY 1967
Bengtsson Zrzavy Orm
KŘÍŽOVÁ DÁMA
Vojtěch Zamarovský Na počátku byl Sumer
Zóna smrti
FUTBAL
ANTOLOGIE AMERICKÉ LITERATURY

BOOK PILLAR INSTALLATION, MUNICIPAL LIBRARY

Mariánské Square, Old Town

At the top of the stairs of the foyer in this otherwise bland building is a sculptural installation by the artist Matej Kren (b. 1958). He was actually born in Bratislava (now in Slovakia) and considers himself Czechoslovakian, rather than Czech. The sculpture consists of a cylindrical stack of books with a large gap in the centre. The viewer is required to place their head inside the gap and look down. Through the careful placing of mirrors, the viewer sees an endless cylinder of these books, as though looking down a well.

PAŘÍŽSKÁ

Old Town

Inspired by Baron Haussmann's redevelopment of Paris in the mid-nineteenth century, Prague's city planners destroyed much of the old Jewish ghetto in the 1890s as part of an urban regeneration scheme. The central diagonal street axis is named Pařížská (Paris Street) with many of the buildings being designed in the prevalent French style of the time, a kind of eclecticism that combined Art Nouveau with historicist elements of older architectural styles such as Gothic and Neoclassicism. Today the street is home to many world-famous retail brands.

SPANISH SYNAGOGUE

Vězeňská, Josefov

Despite the urban regeneration of the late nineteenth century in Josefov, most of the original synagogues remain, together with the Old Jewish Cemetery. The Spanish Synagogue was built in the nineteenth century but on the site of the very first one in Prague, which dated from the eleventh century. Its name refers to the Moorish architectural style seen in such buildings as the Alhambra in Granada, Spain. Today the building is home to a permanent exhibition of Jewish life in Bohemia.

MAISEL SYNAGOGUE

Maiselova, Josefov

The Maisel Synagogue was originally erected in the sixteenth century, at a time of religious toleration in Prague under Rudolph II. It was named after its original benefactor, Mordecai Maisel (1528–1601), the mayor of the Jewish Quarter in Prague. Although rebuilt several times, its latest incarnation dates from the early twentieth century and is now part of the Jewish Museum. In the daytime, visitors can interact with various displays of Jewish historical culture, including a large screen reconstruction of the ghetto, while in the evening the venue provides an atmospheric auditorium for recitals and performances.

TÝNSKÁ ULIKA

Old Town

This is a narrow street in the Old Town in the shadow of the Church of Our Lady before Týn, which takes its name from an enclosed courtyard (Týn) where, from the twelfth century, merchants from foreign lands would pay their customs duties for the merchandise brought into the city. The reason for the enclosure was to protect both the merchants and their goods. The area was also known as the Cheerful Courtyard, where merchants would spend the evenings in taverns exchanging tales of their journeys and adventures along the way.

MAITREA
RESTAURACE
atipico
Le Saint-Tropez
RESTAURANT

DALÍ
Jan& Kája SAUDEK
exhibition
WARHOL
RESTAURANT
CAFFE - RISTORANTE
U TÝNA restaurant & café
PRAGUE SPECIALITIES
ORIGINAL CZECH BEER
RESTAURANT U TÝNA

U TÝNA CAFÉ

Old Town Square, Old Town

This is one of several cafés along the east side of the Old Town Square dominated by the Church of Our Lady before Týn in the background (*see* page 14). The building is in fact medieval and originally comprised of two Gothic houses. In the eighteenth century a Renaissance façade was added. The building is often referred to as the House at the White Unicorn, as it was once owned by an apothecary, whose sign of trade was the mythical beast. Inside, aside from the café is the Galerie d'Art de Prague, which has changing exhibitions of nineteenth- and twentieth-century art.

CHOCO-STORY CHOCOLATE MUSEUM

Celetná, Old Town

The Choco-Story Prague is one of four sites worldwide that tells the story of chocolate from its earliest use by the Mayans about 2,500 years ago, through its appropriation by the Spanish conquistadors into Europe and how it is manufactured and used today. To lure you into the museum is the offer of 'as much chocolate as you can eat' while on the premises, and there are demonstrations and workshops by chocolatiers detailing how to make, for example, truffles. There are also workshops for children and school groups.

CHRISTMAS MARKET

Old Town Square, Old Town

One of three major Christmas markets in the centre of Prague – the other two being in Wenceslas Square and the castle – the Old Town Square market offers the visitor a true sense of a winter wonderland with its brightly lit stalls offering seasonal gifts. The square is dominated by a huge illuminated Christmas tree, and there is a full sized Nativity scene on display. For the children there is a stable with festive animals, such as donkeys and sheep, that can be petted. The markets run from the beginning of December until the beginning of January.

NEOCLASSICAL WIMMER FOUNTAIN

Coal Market, Old Town

Commissioned by the wealthy entrepreneur Jakub Wimmer (1754–1822), the fountain was created by the Czech sculptor František Xaver Lederer (1758–1811) in 1797. It was moved three times from its original location at Wimmer's own palace and is currently in the National Museum Lapidarium building due to continuous vandalism. The one now on display in the Coal Market is a copy. The monument depicts a boy and a girl holding a bunch of grapes, a probable reference to Wimmer's vast estates that included the old medieval royal vineyards.

BASILICA OF ST JAMES

Malá Štupartská, Old Town

The very long nave of this church provides wonderful acoustics for the many concerts held here. The present church in the Baroque style replaced the original, which was destroyed in the great fire of 1689 that decimated the city. One of the main features of the church is its magnificent organ, designed by the Czech organist Abraham Starka, with over 8,000 pipes. Second only to St Vitus Cathedral in size, this basilica – with its 20 altars – is probably the most ornate of all the Baroque churches in Prague.

SVATÁ ANEŽKA ČESKÁ

OLD NEW SYNAGOGUE

Maiselova, Josefov

The oldest surviving and functioning synagogue in Europe, no one really knows how the Old New Synagogue acquired its name, although some believe that angels brought the foundation stones from the Temple in Jerusalem. One of the most remarkable features of the interior is the chair of the former chief Rabbi Judah Loew (1525–1609), an advisor to the liberal-minded Holy Roman Emperor Rudolph II. Loew is also known for his creation of a Golem from the clay basin of the Vltava River, a supposedly anthropomorphic figure that is hidden somewhere in the synagogue.

JEWISH TOWN HALL AND HIGH SYNAGOGUE

Maiselova, Josefov

Another building founded by the Jewish philanthropist Mordecai Maisel was the Jewish Town Hall, erected in 1577. However, the façade was added from 1754 to include the clock tower. There are two dials to the clock: one is a conventional face with Roman numerals, while the one below appears with Hebrew letters that correspond to numbers. So, for example, the first letter of the Hebrew alphabet is *aleph*, which corresponds to the number one. The *aleph* character is, however, located at the conventional number eleven position because the clock hands travel in an anti-clockwise direction.

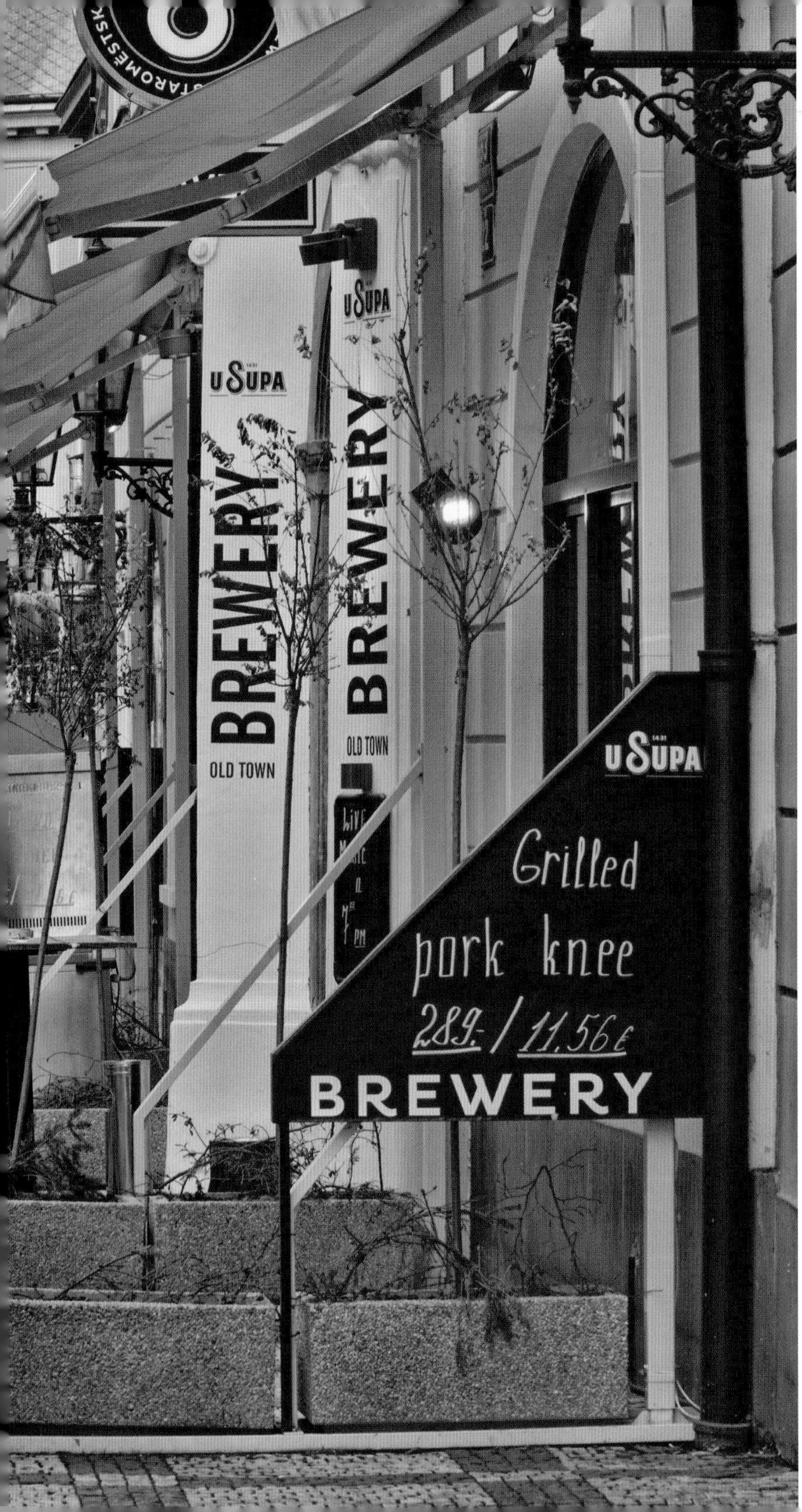

U SUPA BREWERY AND RESTAURANT

Celetná, Old Town

Close to the main campus of Charles University is the oldest continuous brewery in Prague, dating from the fifteenth century. The interior of the house, formerly known as the House of the Vulture, has vaulted ceilings that provide an atmospheric setting for sampling the beers and indulging in the gastronomic delights of Czech cuisine. One of Europe's most respected master brewers, Ivan Chramosil, runs the brewery. It is possible for visitors to see the brewing process in operation through specially constructed glass vats within the restaurant complex.

STORCH HOUSE

Old Town Square, Old Town

On the south side of Old Town Square is the Storch House, which like many of its neighbours has an elegant Renaissance façade. The most notable feature of the façade is the mural of St Wenceslas on horseback. Wenceslas, a Duke of Bohemia, but posthumously created king, was created a saint very soon after his murder in 935. His subsequent legacy in Bohemia and elsewhere was to be seen as a 'righteous king', one who was both a powerful ruler and yet merciful to his enemies.

OBNOVENO L.P. 1948
B. OHMANN - R. KRIEGHAMMER
ARCHITEKTI PROJEKTOVALI L.P. 1897
ARCHITEKT · ING. PRSKAVEC
SVATÝ VÁCLAVE
VÉVODO ČESKÉ ZEMĚ
PROS ZA NÁS

PINKAS SYNAGOGUE

Široká, Josefov

Named after its founder Rabbi Pinkas Horowitz in 1479, the building has undergone many changes in its 500-year existence. It is used today both as a place of worship and as a part of the Jewish Museum. In the upper part of the synagogue is a permanent exhibition of drawings made by children while they were internees at the Nazi Terezín Concentration camp during the Second World War. On the wall of the synagogue itself is a memorial to the 77,000 victims of Terezín who were subsequently deported to various extermination camps.

DETAIL ON HOUSE AT THE TWO BEARS

Melantrichova, Old Town

A beautiful Renaissance house façade that depicts two bears either side of its arched doorway. Facing each of them is a man in armour offering a leafy branch. In medieval times the bear symbolized all that was cruel and savage. By the Renaissance period, it was realized that man through his superior intelligence could tame bears. The allegory here is of two forces, the bear representing the warrior class which if left alone could be tyrannical and brutal, whereas if tamed could be a force for justice and freedom.

BETHLEHEM CHAPEL

Old Town

Originally built between 1391 and 1394, this chapel was used by Jan Hus and his followers who wanted to proclaim the faith in their native Czech language, instead of the more conventional Latin Mass promoted by the Catholic Church. With the eventual execution of Hus and the suppression of the Hussites, the Jesuits acquired the chapel, using it as a storage facility rather than a place of worship. In the eighteenth century it was converted into residential use but fell into disrepair until the 1950s, when it was restored by reference to old illustrations.

ST AGNES CONVENT

U Milosrdných, Old Town

Princess Agnes (1211–82) was the sister of King Wenceslas I (1205–53), with whom she founded the convent that bears her name in 1234. She was an early follower of St Francis of Assisi (1181–1226), who had founded the women's order of the Poor Clares. The church and associated buildings were among the first to be built in Prague in the Gothic style, but became disused in the late eighteenth century after they were closed by King Joseph II. Today the convent has been restored and is used to house the National Gallery of Art's collection.

11
CAFE
TRAMVAJ
2077
CAFE
1429

NEW TOWN, VINOHRADY AND ŽIŽKOV

Despite its name, 'New Town' in Prague was established in 1348 by King Charles IV. Originally it was planned as three central market-places for cattle, hay and horses. Today they are known respectively as Charles Square, Senovážné Square and, the most famous of all, Wenceslas Square. Inhabited mainly by tradespeople and craftsmen in the Middle Ages, much of the New Town was demolished in the nineteenth century to make way for grander buildings in the Neoclassical and Art Nouveau styles that include the National Theatre and the Hlavní Nádraží, Prague's main railway station.

The area of New Town is approximately twice that of Old Town, and has a number of parklands including the Botanical Gardens, which cover over 3.2 ha (8 ac). Here it is possible to taste and buy Czech wines in St Klára's vineyard (*see* page 186). There is also the serpentine-shaped Fata Morgana greenhouse with its three separate temperate zones. Charles Square has a central parkland area laid out in the nineteenth century with lawns, floral displays and fountains.

This chapter also covers the eastern suburbs of Prague just beyond the New Town that include Žižkov and Vinohrady.

CHURCH OF SAINTS CYRIL AND METHODIUS

Resslova, New Town

It seems appropriate that Czechs seeking sanctuary would do so in the church of Saints Cyril and Methodius, two 'Apostles to the Slavs'. In 1942 members of the Czech resistance in Prague assassinated the acting Reich Protector of Bohemia, Reinhard Heydrich (1904–42), during the Nazi occupation. After fleeing the scene they found sanctuary in the crypt of this church, until a Czech traitor betrayed them. The Nazis subsequently murdered all of those involved, including the Bishop of Prague, along with over 1,000 randomly selected Czechs. There is a museum in the church's crypt relating the story.

GRÖBE VILLA

Havlíček Gardens, Vinohrady

Moritz Gröbe (1828–91) was a wealthy industrialist who helped create the railway system in nineteenth-century Bohemia. During the 1870s he commissioned the building of a summer residence for himself on the site of some vineyards that had been there since the fourteenth century. Retaining some of the vineyards, his villa was carefully constructed in a Renaissance style to reflect his tastes, with work by many of the leading designers and craftsmen of the time such as Josef Schulz (1840–1917), under the direction of the architect Antonín Barvitius (1823–1901).

HAVLÍČEK GARDENS

Havlíčkovy Sady, Vinohrady

Havlíček Park was named as such when it was opened to the public for the first time in 1906. Prior to that it was part of the estate belonging to the Gröbe Villa (*see* above and left), complete with the still-used vineyards on its park slopes. The Italian Renaissance-inspired grounds, the fountains, water cascades and the grotto at the northern edge of the park are well worth exploring. At the base of the grotto is a small pool and fountains, as shown here. The Grébovka Pavilion garden café is also worth a visit.

STATUE OF ST WENCESLAS

Wenceslas Square, New Town

This enormous statue of St Wenceslas towers above the street at one end of Wenceslas Square. 'Square' is a misnomer, as it is 750 m (2,461 ft) long and only 60 m (197 ft) wide. The statue was erected in 1912 and created by Josef Václav Myslbek (1848–1922), having taken him over 20 years to complete. Just out of view, on the plinth that supports the equestrian figure, are four other patron saints of the Czech state: Ludmila (the grandmother of Wenceslas), Agnes, Prokop and Adalbert (a former Bishop of Prague).

NATIONAL MUSEUM

Wenceslas Square, New Town

Although founded in 1818, the National Museum did not move into its current location in Wenceslas Square until 1891. Located just behind the statue of Wenceslas, its design resembles that of a Renaissance Palace, particularly on the inside where the focal point is known as the 'Pantheon'. The museum houses a large collection of natural history objects, the National Library, the Czech Museum of Music and the Historical Museum. The building was badly damaged during the Second World War and again during the occupation of Prague in 1968, but has subsequently been restored.

CAFÉ LOUVRE

Národní, New Town

A beautifully restored and elegant interior to this café and restaurant awaits the visitor, after it was badly desecrated by the Communist regime in 1948. Prior to that it had been a popular meeting place since its opening in 1902 for many of the leading intelligentsia of the period, including Albert Einstein (1879–1955) and Franz Kafka. Apart from the café, which resembles a Viennese coffee house, there is a games room that includes several billiard and pool tables. In the summer the café opens the outdoor terrace for its visitors.

NATIONAL THEATRE

Národní, New Town

The original theatre on this site was opened in the summer of 1881 with the premiere of Smetana's opera *Libuše*. However, two months later it was largely destroyed by fire. This was considered such a catastrophic blow to the image of Czech nationalism that its citizens managed to raise enough money almost immediately to rebuild the theatre. The roof of the building is decorated with stars, symbolizing the aspiration of its performers. To the rear of the theatre is a second auditorium added in the 1980s as part of a major refurbishment.

זה השער ליי צדיקים יבאו בו

JERUSALEM SYNAGOGUE

Jeruzalemska, New Town

Originally called the Jubilee Synagogue to commemorate the golden jubilee of Emperor Franz Josef I, who had become King of Bohemia in 1848, it was changed to the Jerusalem Synagogue following the collapse of the Austro-Hungarian Empire and rise of Czech independence. The building, completed in 1906, is a wonderful fusion of Moorish and Art Nouveau styles that come together in the largest synagogue in Prague. Aside from being a place of worship, there is also a permanent exhibition on display called 'The Jewish Community of Prague from 1945 to the Present Day'.

MUCHA MUSEUM

Panská, New Town

Alphonse Mucha is arguably the most well known Czech artist, as well as being at the forefront of the Art Nouveau movement. He is best known for his advertising posters for commercial products and his interior murals, such as those painted at Prague's Municipal House (*see* page 19). 'The Slav Epic', a series of 20 large-scale works painted between 1910 and 1928, depict the history and mythology of the Slavic nations, and are on permanent display. The Mucha Museum is dedicated to the work of the artist and has over 300 works on display.

PALACKÝ BRIDGE

Vltava River, New Town

This view is taken from Palacký Square looking across the Vltava towards the district of Smíchov, famous for its Staropramen Brewery, the second largest in the Czech Republic. The Smíchov district became one of the centres

of industrialization in Prague during the nineteenth century and the bridge was built in 1876 to accommodate the huge increase in traffic, making it the second oldest surviving crossing of the Vltava after the Charles Bridge (*see* page 22).

The bridge is made from granite and was originally decorated with statues from Czech mythology, which were damaged during the Second World War and placed in Vyšehrad Park once restored.

ANTONÍN DVOŘÁK MUSEUM

Ke Karlovu, New Town

If Smetana is the father of Czech music, then Antonín Dvořák (1841–1904) was his disciple, and like him was inspired by Czech culture and nationalism. After early success in Prague, Dvořák moved to the United States where he composed his best known work, Symphony No. 9: 'The New World', which cemented his global appeal, then and now. He returned to Prague in 1895, resuming his post as Professor of Music at the Conservatory until his death in 1904. The Dvořák Museum houses many of his original manuscripts and his piano.

LEGION BRIDGE

Vltava River, New Town

The Legion Bridge spans the Vltava, linking the New Town district with the Lesser Town on the west bank. Crossing the bridge from the latter to the former, one sees the spectacular National Theatre (*see* page 70). While walking in the other direction, the view to the right takes in its neighbour, the Charles Bridge and the castle perched high on the hill, beyond. The bridge is named after the Czech Legion, a group of soldiers fighting for independence from the Austro-Hungarian Empire by siding with the Entente Powers in the First World War.

NEW TOWN HALL

Karlovo Square, New Town

Built as part of the New Town development by Charles IV in 1348, the upper gallery at the top of the tower, almost 70 m (230 ft) high, offers spectacular views of Prague including Charles Square (*see* page 80) which is close by. In 1419 the Town Hall witnessed the first defenestration in Prague at the start of the Hussite Wars. Today, as well as being an administrative office for the area, the building is a cultural centre and offers a history of the New Town as well as a changing exhibition programme.

CHARLES SQUARE

New Town

Originally a livestock market, Charles Square was transformed into a public open green space with seating in the nineteenth century. It is the largest square in Prague with a good variety of trees that include a *ginkgo biloba* and even a magnificent London Plane tree. There are also several sculptural monuments to Czech figures, such as the scientist Jan Purkyně (1787–1869) and the one shown here of the writer Vítězslav Hálek (1835–74). Behind the statue is the municipal courthouse of Prague, which adjoins the New Town Hall.

LUCERNA PALACE

Štěpánská, New Town

A *tour de force* of the Art Nouveau style, this building was erected in 1920, many years after the style became fashionable. The 'palace' is in fact a shopping mall that contains a number of antique shops, several bars and restaurants and even a small cinema. It is also home to the Lucerne Music Bar, a popular jazz and pop music venue. Hanging from the dome inside is a David Černý sculpture of King Wenceslas riding a dead upside-down horse, a satirical comment on today's loss of the Czech identity.

PALLADIUM MALL

Republic Square, New Town

The elegant façade of this shopping centre is in fact an original from the time when the land was an army barracks, which closed in the 1990s. The site was then sold to a developer, creating the largest shopping mall in Prague with a retail space exceeding 37,161 sq m (400,000 sq ft). The upper floors are used for office space. During construction work at the site archaeologists uncovered the remains of a twelfth-century settlement, which suggests that the area around New Town is much older than originally thought.

CAFÉ TRAMVAJ

Wenceslas Square, New Town

In the middle of this famous square, close to Mustek metro station are two old tramcars, complete with track, that have been transformed into an outdoor café with seating and tables below an awning that adjoins the vehicles. The café also provides some indoor seating within the tramcars. The decommissioned vehicles do not look out of place since although Wenceslas Square is not a major thoroughfare for trams, they do cross the square at nearby Vodičkova. The café is an ideal location in which to watch the world go by.

CAFE
TRAMVAJ
11
TAKE AWAY
2077

PRAHA SVÝM VÍTĚZNÝM SYNŮM

PALACKÝ SQUARE

New Town

On the eastern end of Palacký Bridge is a square, both of which are named after the 'Father of the Nation', František Palacký (1798–1876), an eminent historian who was a crucial figure in establishing Czech nationalism in the nineteenth century. The square is dominated on one side by a large memorial to Palacký, who is seen seated, surrounded by creatures representing Heaven and Hell. On the other side is a First World War memorial column dedicated to 'Prague's Victorious Sons'. In the background of the picture is the Emmaus Monastery (*see* page 88) with its twin spires.

CHURCH OF THE MOST SACRED HEART OF OUR LORD

George of Poděbrady Square, Vinohrady

One of only a handful of churches in Prague that is Modernist in style, this one was dedicated to the one-time King of Bohemia, George of Poděbrady (1420–71), the leader of the Hussites who is often credited as the first person to have a vision of European unity. The church was built between 1929 and 1932, and is of a single nave basilica design, with small, high clerestory windows the only source of natural light to illuminate the space. The white marble altar and the large gilded figure of Christ above provide the focal point.

ŠÍTKOVSKÁ WATER TOWER AND NÁPLAVKA RIVERBANK

Rašínovo nábřeží, New Town

The present tower dates from 1591 and supplied most of the drinking water for the city at that time, a service it continued to provide for another 300 years. During the Communist era it was used by the secret police to monitor the movements of the dissident and future first president of the Czech Republic, Václav Havel (1936–2011), who lived in a nearby house. Today the riverside here has an assortment of restaurant barges and a barge hotel, as well as it being the home of Manes Art Restaurant with its huge terraces overlooking the river.

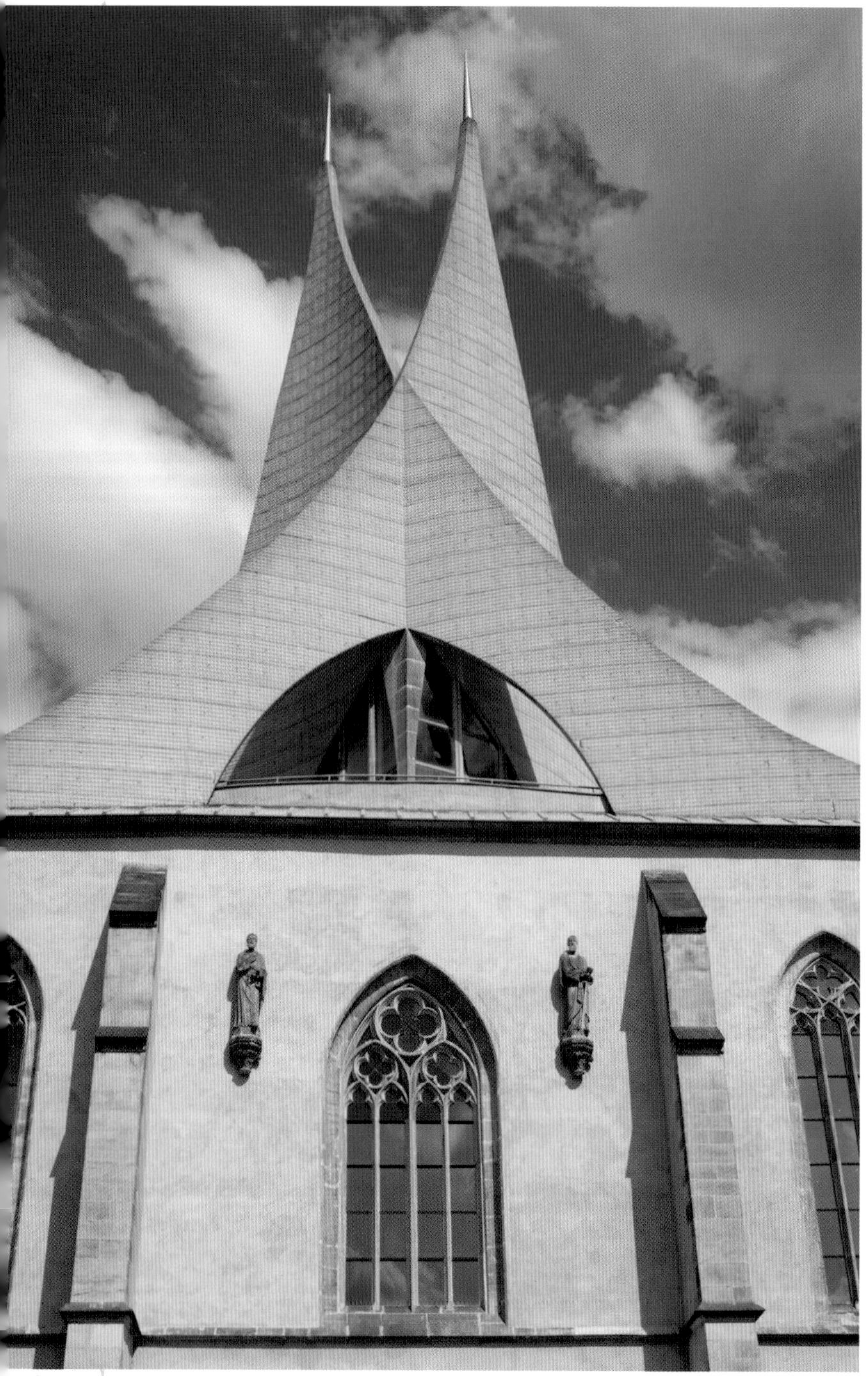

EMMAUS MONASTERY

Vyšehradská, New Town

The one and only Benedictine order monastery in Bohemia was founded here in the fourteenth century and continued until the expulsion of the monks by the Nazis during the Second World War. The buildings were partially destroyed during an accidental bombing by the American air force in 1945, and were then rebuilt in the 1960s when the new roof and unusual double steeples were added. It is currently occupied by a small number of Benedictine monks and continues to function as a monastery.

QUADRIO SHOPPING CENTRE AND THE HEAD OF FRANZ KAFKA

Spálená, New Town

This is an amazing kinetic sculpture in which sections of the head are temporarily displaced during a cyclical routine until they are finally resolved when the head becomes whole again. It is 10 m (33 ft) high and consists of 42 stainless steel individually rotating layers. The work is by the controversial Czech artist David Černý. In many ways the dislocation of the sculptural head reflects many of the ambiguities of Kafka's own mind and his writings that discuss alienation, anxiety and other emotions, often by placing the protagonists in absurd situations.

CAFE LEVEL

DANCING HOUSE

Rašínovo nábřeží, New Town

Affectionately known as the 'Fred and Ginger' building, the Dancing House was commissioned by the Nationale-Nederlanden, a Dutch insurance group, to occupy a vacant site on the riverfront. Its designers were the Czech architect Vlado Milunić (b. 1941) and the Canadian Frank Gehry (b. 1929). Due to its location among several Baroque and Art Nouveau buildings, it was originally seen as controversial, but it did however have the backing of the then Czech president Václav Havel, who had lived in the neighbourhood. It was finally completed in 1996.

CHURCH OF ST LUDMILA

Náměstí míru, Vinohrady

The church is situated on a traffic island known as Míru Square, and is the dominant feature of this area of Prague. It is a Gothic Revival church built in brick with stone detailing and created by the architect Joseph Mocker (1835–99). For the official consecration ceremony in 1892, the relics of St Ludmila were brought here from their normal resting place at St George's Basilica in Prague Castle (*see* page 142). The church has two 60 m (197 ft) steeples that dominate the skyline, the tympanum between containing a large relief of Christ, while the interior is beautifully decorated with colourful frescoes and stained-glass windows.

ST PROCOPIUS CHURCH

Seifertova, Žižkov

Often referred to as the 'Jubilee Church', the foundation stone of St Procopius was laid in 1898, to commemorate the 50th year of the reign of Emperor Franz Joseph I. It was the first church on this site and it was decided to build one here because Žižkov had become an independent city in 1881 and did not have its own Catholic church. As with most Neo-Gothic churches, this one was meant to impress, hence its spire reaching over 70 m (230 ft) and the elaborately carved relief over the north door of the Madonna and Child receiving St Procopius.

CHRISTMAS MARKET

Míru Square, Vinohrady

This view is taken near the Church of St Ludmila looking on to the Christmas market in Míru Square. It is one of the lesser-known Christmas markets in Prague since it is outside the main tourist areas. Nevertheless, it has a full array of handicrafts that make ideal gifts. The wooden logcabin-style stalls also have samples of Czech food, such as open roasted ham and *trdelník*, a hot sweet pastry. Traditional drinks are also on offer, including the famous Czech Pilsners or *svařák*, a mulled wine.

CHURCH OF VIRGIN MARY SNOW AND FRANCISCAN GARDEN

Jungmann Square, New Town

A fourth-century legend tells of a night in August when snow fell on a hill in Rome. Seeing this as a divine act, Pope Liberius (310–66) decreed that a church should be built on the hill and dedicated to the Virgin Mary. One thousand years later a church of the same name was proposed in Prague but was only ever partially completed. It was subjected to damage during the Hussite Wars and was largely rebuilt in the Baroque style. The Franciscan Gardens provide a small oasis within this busy area of the city.

ŽIŽKOV TELEVISION TOWER

Mahlerovy Sady, Žižkov

Having been built in the late Communist era, this television transmission tower was viewed with a great deal of scepticism when it was constructed in 1985. The Prague citizens were also denigrating of the structure because, with utter insensitivity, it had been built on the site of an old Jewish cemetery. Today, however, this 200 m (656 ft) tower, an example of 'high-tech' architecture, is visited by many tourists due to its outstanding views across the city from its viewing platform and restaurant at 90 m (295 ft).

RIEGROVY BEER GARDEN

Riegrovy Park, Vinohrady

During the summer months outdoor drinking is very popular in Prague, and Riegrovy Sady Beer Garden is one of the most popular, particularly as it serves lagers made in microbreweries. Riegrovy Park itself is also home to a number of sporting activities and consequently this drinking hole becomes a popular retreat for participants. It is also very popular with the tourists. There is a range of grilled food on offer and the large projector screen enables patrons to watch major sporting events live.

Gambrinus
Gambrinus

VINOHRADSKÁ

Vinohrady

Over 4 km (2.5 mi) in length, Vinohradská is one of the longest roads in Prague and stretches from the Národní Museum in New Town towards the east. The western end of the street is dominated by retail stores and apartment blocks. This view is from the junction of the street with Izraelská, the New Jewish Cemetery and its gateway on the right. The unusual Post-Modern building on the left is the Health Insurance Ministry, and in the distance on the right is the Žižkov Television Tower (*see* page 98).

NATIONAL MONUMENT AND VITKOV HILL

Žižkov

The view shown here is from the highest point of the National Monument at the top of Vitkov Hill. In the foreground is one of the world's largest equestrian statues, depicting Jan Žižka, a fifteenth-century general who successfully fought in the Hussite Wars at the Battle of Vitkov. The large building beneath houses changing exhibitions but is also the location for the Memorial Tomb of the Unknown Soldier (*see* below and right). The monument was built between 1928 and 1938 to commemorate the Czech soldiers who fell in the First World War, leading to the creation of Czechoslovakia as an independent nation.

MEMORIAL TOMB

Vitkov Hill, Žižkov

The remains of an unidentified soldier were brought to Prague in 1922 after they had been exhumed from the site of the Battle of Zborov that took place in July 1917. The new Czechoslovakian state wanted to remember its First World War dead, but its soldiers had been fighting on both sides of the conflict. The Nazis destroyed the original site of the tomb in Old Town Square, and it was not until the new millennium that these and other remains from soldiers killed in the Second World War were finally interred in the Memorial Tomb.

VINOHRADY THEATRE

Miru Square, Vinohrady

Close to the Church of St Ludmila (*see* page 92) is the Vinohrady Theatre, built at the beginning of the twentieth century and at the time of its construction second in size only to the National Theatre (*see* page 70). It was designed in the Neo-Renaissance style, which is often confused with Art Nouveau, by the architect Alois Čenský (1868–1954). The figures at the top of the building represent Comedy and Tragedy, while the four figures beneath represent Tragedy, Ballet, Comedy and Opera, showing the diversity of the theatre's productions.

JUNGMANN STATUE

Jungmann Square, New Town

Josef Jungmann (1773–1847) was a writer and is credited along with Josef Dobrovský (1753–1829) of developing the modern Czech language as part of the so-called Czech National Revival, a counter to the imperialism of German under the Austro-Hungarian Empire. Jungmann's contribution was to produce the first German-Czech dictionary, published between 1834 and 1839. The location of the named square and adjoining street, Jungmannova, close to Wenceslas Square, is significant as both are linked to Czech identity and culture. The square was named in 1876 when the statue to Jungmann was also unveiled.

FRANZ KAFKA'S GRAVE

New Jewish Cemetery, Vinohrady

When the Old Jewish Cemetery and much of Josefov was cleared at the end of the nineteenth century, a new cemetery was opened in 1890 at Vinohrady with a greatly increased capacity. The prevailing style at this time was Art Nouveau and consequently many of the early memorials here are of significant aesthetic merit. There is also a beautiful memorial to the Jewish victims of the Holocaust and, of course, perhaps the best known Jew of modern times, Franz Kafka, who was laid to rest here in 1924.

Dr FRANZ KAFKA
1883–1924
HERMANN KAFKA
1854–1931
JULIE KAFKA
1856–1934
ERNESTINE LEVY

Lennon
hostinec U dvou slunců
ej Bůh štěstí
MALOSTRANSKÁ PIVNICE

LESSER TOWN AND THE CASTLE DISTRICT

Lesser Town, or Little Quarter as it is sometimes known, is the least recently developed area of Prague, with few buildings created in the nineteenth or twentieth centuries. It was originally created at the foot of the Castle District in the late thirteenth century and provides many of the spectacular views across the Vltava towards Old Town, most notably from Charles Bridge (*see* page 22) that links both districts. For today's visitor the key highlights of Lesser Town are the Wallenstein Palace (*see* page 112), initially intended to rival even the Royal Palace, and the magnificent Baroque masterpiece, Church of St Nicholas (*see* page 130). The tranquil Vojan Gardens (*see* page 111) and the much larger and more dynamic Petřín Park provide outdoor spaces to enjoy. The narrow street known as Nerudova (*see* page 148) leading up to the Castle District is also worth exploring.

Of the five central areas of Prague, the Castle District is the oldest, dating from the ninth century. Inside the castle wall are two palaces, the Cathedral of St Vitus (*see* page 136), two other churches and a monastery. The adjoining area, known as Hradčany, has another five palaces and three more monasteries including the Loreto (*see* page 146). Unlike the other four districts, the Castle and Hradčany have no riverside access.

CHURCH OF THE ARCHANGEL MICHAEL

Petřin Hill, Lesser Town

There are two churches in Prague dedicated to St Michael the Archangel, the other being in New Town. The one in Lesser Town was built more recently and is unconventional for two reasons. Following the First World War and the collapse of the Austro-Hungarian Empire, the small historic state of Carpathian Ruthenia was annexed to the new Czechoslovakia in 1919. To mark the tenth anniversary, this small church was erected as an Orthodox Carpathian Ruthenian place of worship. The church is also made entirely of wood and painted in red, green and white, symbolizing love, life and goodness.

VOJAN GARDENS

Wallenstein Palace, Lesser Town

Just along from the bustle of Charles Bridge is the tranquil park known as the Vojan Gardens, hidden behind a very high wall that was originally part of a Carmelite monastery founded in the seventeenth century, although there had been a religious order here in the medieval period. Inside the park are two small chapels, one of which is in the form of a grotto. At one end of the garden is a large terrace with seating and a rose pergola as seen in the picture.

WALLENSTEIN PALACE AND GARDEN

Valdštejnské Square, Lesser Town

This magnificent palace was built for Albrecht von Wallenstein (1583–1634), the supreme commander of the Habsburg armed forces. It was intended to rival the emperor's own palace in the castle precincts. The ceiling of the palace's main hall is painted with a fresco depicting Wallenstein as Mars, the Roman god of war, but his aspirations towards monarchic power were met with hostility and charges of high treason, and he was assassinated. Today the palace is a tourist attraction and the old riding school building is used as an art gallery.

CHURCH OF OUR LADY VICTORIOUS

Karmelitská, Lesser Town

This building is the oldest Baroque church in Prague and dates from 1613 when it was consecrated as the Church of the Holy Trinity for the German Lutherans. Following the Battle of White Mountain in 1620, however, it became a Catholic church, dedicated to the victory over the Hussites. The Baroque splendour of the church's interior is manifest in several altars along the nave, the most notable of which contains the Infant Jesus of Prague, a small statue originally from Spain that is venerated by Christians who visit this church from all over the world.

CAFÉ SAVOY

Vítězná, Lesser Town

A very short walk from the west end of the Legion Bridge is the Café Savoy, an elegant *fin de siècle* interior redolent of many of the coffee and patisserie establishments in Vienna. Sitting here one can easily imagine the intelligentsia gathering to discuss new ideas and current affairs. Today it has lost none of its atmosphere as a busy establishment that offers many Czech specialities, such as warm Prague ham for breakfast, and pork belly and sauerkraut for lunch. There is also a delicious range of pastries made in the café's own bakery.

JOHN LENNON PUB

Hroznová, Lesser Town

Not far from the very famous John Lennon Wall is a public house that also bears his name. On passing through the door, above which is a 'Yellow Submarine' sign, the visitor enters a low ceiling 'cavern' with arches, not dissimilar to the old Cavern Club in Liverpool (now demolished) where the Beatles first performed their music. Beatles music is playing in the background and a large number of British style artefacts, including a replica red telephone box, add to the ambience. The menu is a strange mix of British and Czech cuisine.

JOHN LENNON WALL

Velkopřevorské Square, Lesser Town

One of the most photographed spots in Prague is the so-called John Lennon Wall, created originally in the 1980s by a group of disaffected students during the Communist era. The notion of 'Lennonism' that advocated love and peace was adopted by many who eschewed (Communist and Fascist) tyranny, as well as capitalism. The image shown here has long since disappeared but the wall continues to be decorated by street artists and is a place of pilgrimage for those who follow the basic tenets of 'Lennonism'.

FREE MABOR
ennon
CHELLSEY WOODS 2016
FREEDOM
LARUCAS FOR EVER!
13.3.2015.
MITCHELL SUCKLING 2016.
ALL NEED IS LOVE
Nothing worth having comes easy

OBSERVATION TOWER

Petřín Hill, Lesser Town

The Petřín Hill Observation Tower strongly resembles the Eiffel Tower in Paris and was built in 1891 for the Prague World Fair, after members of the Czech Tourist Club visited the Exposition Universelle in 1889. It differs slightly in structure in that the Eiffel Tower stands on four legs, while the Petřín Tower is hexagonal at the base. Standing at 63 m (207 ft) in height, it is only one-fifth of the height of the Eiffel Tower, but since the Petřín Tower is already built on a high vantage point in Petřín Park it appears much higher.

ST LAWRENCE CHURCH

Petřín Hill, Lesser Town

Almost adjacent to the Observation Tower is the church of St Lawrence that, according to legend, was originally built on a pagan site in the twelfth century. The church was given a Baroque makeover in the eighteenth century and today is a cathedral of the 'Old Catholic' church, which dismisses some doctrines of the Roman Catholic faith, most notably papal authority. Close to the church are the Stations of the Cross, a series of marble altarpieces set at intervals up the hill to represent Calvary that are used during Lent.

PARADISE GARDEN

Palace Complex, Hradčany

Paradise Garden is now incorporated into what are called the South Gardens, a narrow strip of land along the southern ramparts of the castle, overlooking Lesser Town. Paradise Garden is the oldest of them. It was originally the private garden of King Ferdinand I and of Rudolph II in the sixteenth century. The current layout of the garden dates from the 1920s. This view is from the terrace of the garden overlooking Lesser Town, which is dominated by the green domed basilica of St Nicholas.

SEMINARY GARDEN

Petřín Park, Lesser Town

The garden, on the eastern side of Petřín Park, was originally called the Gryspek when it was a Carmelite monastery in the seventeenth century, but was given its current name when it became a theological college (seminary) under the control of an archbishop. Originally there were many fruit trees planted here, some of which still survive, making it a pleasant place to visit in the spring when the blossom is evident. The garden was taken over in the early twentieth century by the municipal authority and opened to the public.

PETŘÍN FUNICULAR RAILWAY

Petřín Hill, Lesser Town

Petřín Hill is nearly 305 m (1,000 ft) above the city and can be climbed by a series of steps. Most people, however, take the funicular railway to the top. Built to take passengers to the Observation Tower as part of the Prague World Fair in 1891 (*see* page 118), it was originally powered by water pressure until 1914 when it was converted to electric power. The railway has two stops. The first, which is about halfway up, is for the Nebozízek Restaurant with fabulous views over Prague, and the second is for the Observation Tower.

MÁNES BRIDGE

Vltava River, Lesser Town

Charles Bridge's neighbour to the north is the Mánes crossing, designed and built during the First World War and originally named the Archduke Bridge, after the emperor. Following the death of the emperor and subsequent loss of the empire, the bridge was renamed after the Czech academic painter Josef Mánes (1820–71), whose statue is at the Old Town end of the crossing. Mánes is most famous for his painting of the dial face on the Astronomical Clock on the Old Town Hall between 1864 and 1866 (*see* page 18).

KAMPA ISLAND

Lesser Town

Kampa takes its name from the Latin *campus*, meaning a field. The term was applied to this island 'field' that had been artificially created to power watermills by digging a narrow canal waterway fed from, and back into, the Vltava. The canal was known as the Devil's Stream in the nineteenth century because of the abusive behaviour of a local resident nearby. Although there are remnants and reminders of its past use, today the island is used purely as a leisure facility with pubs, bars and a tranquil park, and is often referred to as the 'Venice of Prague'.

VRTBA GARDEN

Karmelitská, Lesser Town

On the northern slope of Petřín Hill is this exquisite Baroque garden, created for the Count of Vrtba, as part of his palace between 1715 and 1720. The terrace seen here on the left takes the visitor down to the garden by way of a series of interconnecting stairways graced with sculptures in true Baroque style. The palace was altered considerably in the nineteenth century to the Neoclassical style, and although the garden was altered as well, it has subsequently been returned to its former Baroque glory.

KAMPA ISLAND MILL

Kampa Island, Lesser Town

This is one of three mills that survive intact, along the Devil's Stream. The jetty was used at one time for the narrow boats to take the milled grain out on to the river. The former mill building has been transformed into the Studio Velkopřevorský Mlýn, a series of boutique studio apartments for short-term rental. The front of the property opens up on to the Velkopřevorské Square where the John Lennon wall is located. Across the stream is the Velkopřevorský Mlýn restaurant with an outside balcony and seating overlooking the stream.

LOVERS' BRIDGE

Čertovka, Kampa Island, Lesser Town

Just along from the former mill is the Lovers' Bridge, linking the street Hroznová to Velkopřevorské Square. This narrow walking bridge is very crowded with couples using the background as a photo opportunity. As with many other Lovers' Bridges around the world, this one has a number of padlocks fixed to its railings. They are symbolic of unbroken love, as a couple usually throws the key into the water below after fixing the padlock. The tradition began about a century ago in Eastern Europe and has now become a global phenomenon.

CHURCH OF ST NICHOLAS

Malostranské Square, Lesser Town

Arguably the most sumptuous Baroque church in Prague, with three generations of the same family working on its construction, which by 1752 had taken about 50 years to complete. The original church on the site, also dedicated to St Nicholas, had been there since the thirteenth century. The replacement church is lavishly decorated on the inside with the finest Baroque statuary, most particularly the huge gilded statue of St Nicholas above the high altar. High above this is the domed ceiling with a fresco by František Xaver Palko (1724–67).

KAMPA MUSEUM

U Sovových Mlýnů, Lesser Town

The building now occupied by the Kampa Museum was originally Sova Mill, which backed directly on to the Vltava. The museum was opened by Dr Meda Mládková (b. 1919) in 2003 to display the large collection of Central European art that she and her late husband had collected. Mládková returned to Prague after the Velvet Revolution, following her exile in Western Europe. Today the gallery remains dedicated to contemporary art, mainly by Czech artists. As one approaches the gallery entrance, there are a number of sculptures displayed outside including *The Rider* by Michal Gabriel (b. 1960) of 2008–09.

NA KAMPĚ

Kampa Island, Lesser Town

This view of the street called Na Kampě is taken from the Charles Bridge. At this point it is possible to descend the staircase alongside the bridge to gain entry to the street that continues into the large open green space at the centre of Kampa Island. Along the street one can seek shade from the hot summer sun with seating provided under the central avenue of trees. On either side of this pedestrianized street are several shops, cafés and some market stalls selling local handicrafts.

PRAGUE CASTLE

Palace Complex, Hradčany

This evening view from a high vantage point in the Old Town shows the Castle District to the right, illuminated as always at night. In the centre of the picture is the Church of St Nicholas (*see* page 130) with its green dome and adjacent bell tower. There are many such vantage points around

the city, as the castle is on high ground, but the most awe-inspiring are those close to the river when the reflections of the illuminations add to the spectacle. The best of these is from Smetanovo nábřeží that includes the Charles Bridge, which is also illuminated.

ST VITUS CATHEDRAL

Palace Complex, Hradčany

In 925, Wenceslas was presented with the partial relic of St Vitus as a sacred gift which he then enshrined by building a rotunda on this site, dedicated to the martyr. Ten years later Wenceslas himself was also buried here after his martyrdom. The rotunda has long since gone but it is replaced by one of the most spectacular cathedrals in Europe, high up within the castle precincts. It contains many masterpieces, including the richly decorated Chapel of St Wenceslas and the silver funerary monument of St John of Nepomuk.

GOLDEN LANE

Palace Complex, Hradčany

The alternative name for this charming little street is Alchemists' Lane, since legend suggests it was here that alchemists were charged with finding the Philosopher's Stone, a method of turning base metals into gold, by their patron King Rudolph II (1552–1612). During the nineteenth century one side of the street was demolished, and it was during the twentieth century that the houses were given a makeover and painted in bright colours. Two famous writers lived in Golden Lane in the twentieth century: Franz Kafka, who wrote some of his short stories here, and the Nobel Laureate Jaroslav Seifert (1901–86).

ROYAL GARDEN

Prague Castle, Hradčany

On the north side of the castle complex, where at one time a defensive moat was sited, a formal garden was created in the middle of the sixteenth century for King Ferdinand I. The king also commissioned the building of the Belvedere Palace at one end of the garden as a summer retreat for his wife Anne. The palace with its loggia is one of the finest examples of Renaissance architecture outside Italy. In front of the palace is the famous 'Singing Fountain', by Tomáš Jaroš (1500–71).

ČERNÍN PALACE

Loretánské Square, Hradčany

This 152 m (500 ft) long palace that has no less than 30 massive Corinthian columns on its façade is a truly imposing site on the square. It was built for Count Černín (1628–82), an imperial ambassador, to reflect his status and wealth. The French damaged the palace during the Siege of Prague in 1742, which led to some of the interiors being refurbished in a Rococo style. With the birth of Czechoslovakia in 1918, the palace became the Ministry of Foreign Affairs, a function it still performs today.

STRAHOV LIBRARY

Strahov Monastery, Hradčany

The library, which is part of the Strahov Monastery, is often known as the Theological Hall, completed in 1679 under the direction of the Abbot Jeroným Hirnheim (1637–79), himself a leading theologian. Siard Nosecký (1693–1753) painted the ceiling roundels in the eighteenth century. After the Second World War and during the Communist era the library became state property and was incorporated into the Memorial of National Literature. Following the Velvet Revolution it has been returned to the monks and contains over 5,000 manuscripts, as well as examples of Czech literature from the ninth century.

BASILICA OF THE ASSUMPTION OF OUR LADY

Strahov Monastery, Hradčany

Next door to the Philosophical and Theological Halls is the magnificent Basilica of the Assumption of Our Lady. It was rebuilt several times since its first incarnation in the twelfth century, and today is largely Baroque in style. The church comprises a nave and two side aisles, which are decorated with scenes of the life of St Norbert, the founder of the Premonstratensian Order to which the monastery of Strahov belongs. It is known that Mozart himself played the former organ in this church.

ST GEORGE'S BASILICA

Palace Complex, Hradčany

The unusual coloured façade of this church was created in the seventeenth century as part of a Baroque makeover. In fact, the church is one of the oldest in Prague and was originally built in the tenth century, housing the remains of the murdered St Ludmila, grandmother of St Wenceslas. Behind the façade are two white towers, one called Adam, the other Eve, which are, like most of the church, twelfth-century Romanesque. The interior, too, has all the hallmarks of the Romanesque style with its thick heavy walls, rounded arches and small clerestory windows.

ARCHBISHOP'S PALACE

Hradčany Square

Although having the appearance of a Rococo palace, behind the elaborate façade is a more modest Renaissance building given to the Archbishop of Prague in 1562 by King Ferdinand I. With its proximity to the royal palace, the 'gift' was intended to signify the closeness of the monarch, as Holy Roman Emperor, to the official Catholic Church as part of the Counter-Reformation. The Throne Room is decorated with the finest Gobelins tapestries from France. The palace is used by the current archbishop and is not open to the public.

ČERNÍN GARDEN

Loretánské Square, Hradčany

Since 2011 the garden behind the Černín Palace has been open to the public. It was created in 1693, about 11 years after Count Černín had died, and remained in the hands of his descendants. Like the palace, the garden was damaged by the French in 1742 and then again by the Prussians in 1757. However, the garden was restored and a new summerhouse was built in 1774. Subsequently it has been restored another three times, the most recent being between 1994 and 1997.

LORETO CHURCH

Loreto Square, Hradčany

An important place of pilgrimage, the Loreto is one of the most visited holy sites in central Europe, and was created as part of the Catholic Counter-Reformation. The main chapel, the Santa Casa, promoted the legend of Santa Casa in Loreto, a small town in Italy that is the site of the Virgin Mary's house where she received word of the Assumption. During the Crusades, the house was supposedly transported by angels from the Holy Land to Loreto. The church contains many valuable treasures, including the gold monstrance for holding the Eucharistic host.

LEDEBURSKÁ GARDEN

Palace Complex, Hradčany

The garden is on the southern slope of the castle walls and is now a series of terraced spaces with Baroque staircases taking the visitor to the different levels. In the medieval period these gardens were vineyards, but today they provide a quiet oasis away from the hustle and bustle of the tourist area. Each level provides planting and statuary as it would have appeared in the seventeenth century when an aristocratic family owned it. Today the garden can be enjoyed by everyone and it provides wonderful views across Prague.

EXCHANGE & HOTEL
hostinec U dvo
OBCHOD
LOUTKAMI
47
SUVENÝRY
U
DVOU SLUNCŮ
Pilsner Urquell

NERUDOVA

Lesser Town

This charming narrow street leading from Lesser Town to the castle precincts was originally on the royal coronation route from Charles Bridge. The street is named after the writer Jan Neruda (1834–91) who occupied one of these houses and wrote a number of short stories about the area. His house had the emblem of the Two Suns, and many others have characters rather than numbers to distinguish them, such as the Red Eagle and the Green Lobster. There are also two grand buildings in this street that were former palaces and are now used as foreign embassies.

TRADITIONAL PUB

Cihelná, Lesser Town

Based on the style of a typical old Czech pub, the Malostranská Pivnice is in fact a restaurant with over 250 covers inside and 200 tables in the courtyard for summer use. The main restaurant building dates from 1847 and was at one time the home of a leading art historian, Anna Masaryková (1911–96). The restaurant was opened in 2003 and serves traditional Czech food and a good range of local beers, for which Bohemia is famed. The most famous of these are the original Budweiser, Staropramen and Pilsner Urquell.

FRANZ KAFKA MUSEUM
FRANZ KAFKA MUSEUM
Franz Kafka Museum
Franz Kafka Museum

FRANZ KAFKA MUSEUM

Cihelná, Lesser Town

Formerly the Herget Brickworks, this building has been home to the Kafka Museum since 2005, with a permanent exhibition entitled 'The City of Franz Kafka and Prague'. It is divided into two sections. First, the 'Existential Space' relates how Prague influenced Kafka's writing, leading to him seeing the city as 'a dear little mother with claws'. The second section is called 'Imaginary Topography', because in his writing Kafka did not specifically name locations, instead creating a city that is actually beyond Realism.

MEMORIAL TO THE VICTIMS OF COMMUNISM

Újezd, Lesser Town

With its obvious homage to the human forms of the sculptor Alberto Giacometti (1901–66), the Czech artist Olbram Zoubek (1926–2017) created this memorial to the victims of Communism which was unveiled in 2002, 12 years after the Velvet Revolution and the fall of the Communist regime. The catatonic figures appear more broken and disjointed the further away one views them, with the bronze strip between them relating the numbers actually affected – in excess of a third of a million people – either arrested, jailed, exiled or murdered between 1948 and 1989.

HOLEŠOVICE, VYŠEHRAD AND BEYOND

In the outlying districts of central Prague are a number of significant cultural locations to be explored. They are Vyšehrad in the south, Hvězda and Břevnov in the west, and Dejvice, Troja and Holešovice in the north.

Historically the most important of these is Vyšehrad, which means 'Castle on the Heights' and is by tradition the oldest part of the city, according to the legend of Libuše, who foretold of Prague's greatness. Archaeology reveals that the first castle was, however, built on this rocky outcrop in the tenth century. The ruins of Libuše's Baths still exist, which were in fact part of the medieval defences of the castle. It is perhaps significant that this ancient settlement has since the nineteenth century been the final resting place of many famous Czech nationals.

Two large parkland areas, Letná (*see* page 154) and Stromovka (*see* page 160), dominate the district of Holešovice. The former is home to one of the most dominating and strange sculptures, the Prague Metronome (*see* page 158) and the quirky Hanavský Pavilion (*see* page 156), while Stromovka Park is the site of the wonderful Art Nouveau Industrial Palace (*see* page 161), with its Křižík Fountain (*see* page 162), which to this day is a cultural venue.

LETNÁ PARK

Czechia, Holešovice

From the north-west end of the Čechův Bridge (*see* page 13), one can access Letná Park by climbing the 200 plus steps to get to the summit, with all the while the huge metronome in view. From the summit there are magnificent views of the Vltava, its bridges and most of the city of Prague. The park is well suited to outdoor activities such as jogging and skateboarding, and has a large beer garden in the west, the perfect spot in the summer to view the city and to drink ice-cold Czech Pilsner.

LETNÁ WATER TOWER

Holešovice

Built in 1888 in the Romanesque style, the Letná Water Tower was one of several built in the city to provide fresh water for its citizens. This one contains a cylinder with a capacity of 204,574 l (45,000 gal) to supply water for the Holešovice district. It was, however, decommissioned as early as 1913 and converted into apartments for use by the water company's employees. Just below the pyramidal apex is a viewing gallery at 21 m (70 ft) that provides an excellent vantage point from the north of Letná Park.

HANAVSKÝ PAVILION

Letná Park, Holešovice

In the east of the park is the Hanavský Pavilion, an impressive Neo-Baroque/Art Nouveau building designed by Otto Hieser (1850–92), an Austrian architect, for the Komárov Ironworks Company for their participation in the 1891 Prague World Fair. The pavilion was originally located in Petřín Park, and in keeping with the company's products it was constructed in cast iron, becoming the first of its kind in Prague. It was relocated after the exposition and is today a well-respected restaurant, its outdoor terrace providing a spectacular view of the Vltava and its bridges.

NATIONAL TECHNICAL MUSEUM

Kostelní, Holešovice

The museum, although founded in 1908, was not established on this site until after the Second World War, having accumulated many artefacts from different collections in the interim. For some time, until the present building was constructed, the museum's collection was held at various locations, including the Schwarzenberg Palace. Under Communist rule the museum continued to provide regular expositions on technical subjects such as mining, transportation and astronomy, but tenants such as the Cartographic Institute also used the large building for other purposes until 1990. Today it is used solely to promote Czech innovation and technical ability.

PRAGUE METRONOME

Letná Park, Holešovice

This 23 m (75 ft) kinetic sculpture sits on top of a huge granite base that was at one time the rock on which a massive statue of Stalin was erected in 1955, a symbol of his grip on the city below. The monument was torn down seven years later during the so-called de-Stalinization of the Soviet regime. The metronome was unveiled in 1992 and serves as a reminder of the oppression that Czechs endured during the Communist period, the red hand of the sculpture making a continuous broad sweep across Prague.

STROMOVKA PARK

Výstaviště, Holešovice

Bordered on its northern edge by the Vltava, Stromovka is the largest of the parks in and around Prague, and is ideally suited for outdoor activities. Its name means the 'place of trees' and it was used as a hunting forest for the royal family before it was opened to the public in 1804. While it was a royal park, two large ponds were dug and these can still be visited as places of tranquillity surrounded by weeping willow trees. To the east of the park is the exhibition ground.

INDUSTRIAL PALACE

Stromovka Park, Výstaviště, Holešovice

The magnificent Art Nouveau Industrial Palace was the centrepiece of the 1891 Prague World Fair. The iron, steel and glass building is divided into three sections: a central hall, above which is the clock tower, and an east and west wing. The exhibition lasted from May to October 1891 and attracted 2.5 million visitors. The building continued to function as an exhibition hall until the Soviets took control when it became the Congress Palace, the meeting place for the Communist Party in Prague. Since 1990 it has been used as a cultural events venue.

KŘIŽÍK FOUNTAIN

Výstaviště, Holešovice

Set behind the Industrial Palace (*see* page 161) is an outdoor arena with amphitheatre-style seating from where to watch the light and water displays of the Křižík Fountain. Opened in 1891 as part of the Prague World Fair, its designer František Křižík (1847–1941), an almost forgotten pioneer of electrical engineering, created a masterpiece of entertainment that was the envy of much of Europe. Today, after considerable refurbishment, the dancing coloured water displays are computer controlled with accompanying music to provide this exceptional spectacle that uses over 3,000 jets for its effects.

ST MATTHEW'S FAIR

Stromovka Park, Výstaviště, Holešovice

The 'Matějská pout' (St Matthew's Pilgrimage) as it is known in Prague, takes place each year on this site starting in early spring. The pilgrimage and its annual festival have taken place for the last 400 years, originally culminating at St Matthew's Church to the north of the city at Dejvice. The pilgrimage today is of a secular nature and involves over 100 attractions, such as roller-coasters, carousels and a Ferris wheel, as seen here. There is also a haunted house and a maze.

PRAGUE PLANETARIUM

Výstaviště, Holešovice

Originally built in 1960, the planetarium makes a welcome addition to the site close to the Industrial Palace (*see* page 161). The equipment has been upgraded twice since then and is now capable of projecting high-resolution images on to the inside of its vast dome, for watching the presentation called 'The Night Sky'. There are a number of programmes to watch, some in English, showing the history of astronomy in Czechoslovakia since the time of King Rudolph II, science's great patron in the seventeenth century.

STATUES AT THE LAPIDARIUM FAÇADE

National Museum – Lapidary, Výstaviště, Holešovice

At the entrance to the Industrial Palace (*see* page 161) is a Renaissance-style villa, also built in 1891 for the Prague World Fair. In one of its wings is the Lapidarium, a satellite of the National Museum (*see* page 68) for the display of sculpture. Its collection of over 2,000 artefacts dates from the eleventh century, but there are usually only 450 of them on display at any time. The most important statues of the permanent display are the original sculptures from the Charles Bridge (*see* page 22), including that of Charles IV and his son Wenceslas IV.

STROSSMAYEROVO SQUARE

Holešovice

The focal point of the square is the Neo-Gothic Church of St Anthony of Padua, consecrated in 1911 after three years' construction. Its overall appearance is not dissimilar to the Church of Our Lady before Týn in Old Town (*see* page 14). The towers, which are nearly 61 m (200 ft) high, each house a bell. The oldest, originally cast in 1572, is in the right tower, and the one on the left is a copy of America's Liberty Bell presented to Tomáš Masaryk, the president of the new Czechoslovakia by the US president, Woodrow Wilson (1856–1924), in 1918.

PĚŠÍ ZÓNA
MHD
ZÁSOBOVÁNÍ

HISTORIC FORT OF VYŠEHRAD

V Pevnosti, Vyšehrad

The district of Vyšehrad lies to the south of the New Town along the east bank of the Vltava, and is by tradition the oldest settlement in Prague, its high vantage point and rocky outcrop well suited to view the river's comings and goings. The early dynastic rulers of Bohemia, the Přemyslids, created the first castle here in the tenth century at a similar time as the citadel at Prague Castle. Between the tenth and early fourteenth centuries the ruling monarchy switched between the two castles as their primary residence.

VYŠEHRAD CEMETERY

K Rotundě, Vyšehrad

Located within the old castle precincts is the Vyšehrad Cemetery. Established in 1869 and containing the Slavin Pantheon, the cemetery was built in 1900 as a final resting place for the most honoured citizens of the city, including Josef Myslbek who sculpted the famous equestrian statue of King Wenceslas, the artist Alphonse Mucha and the genius inventor František Křižík. The cemetery is also the final resting place for the Czech composers Antonín Dvořák and Bedřich Smetana, the international opera singer Emmy Destinn (1878–1930), the poet Jan Neruda and 'Pepi' Bican (1913–2001), one of the most prolific goalscorers in European football.

BASILICA CHURCH OF ST PETER AND ST PAUL

Vyšehrad

The most dominant feature of present day Vyšehrad is the Basilica Church of St Peter and St Paul with its 61 m (200 ft) high spired towers. It is the third church of this name to be built on the site, the first being in the eleventh century. This one was completed in 1903 and is of a basilica design without transepts. Much of the interior is decorated with large frescoes and murals in the predominantly Art Nouveau style, and there are also a number of Baroque paintings from the sixteenth century.

VYŠEHRAD PARK

Štulcova, Vyšehrad

Originally there were no trees at all on this rocky outcrop, a situation that remained unchanged until the middle of the nineteenth century. The small park was created in 1927–28, on the site of the original royal palace. Inside the park are four sculptural groups created in 1948 by the leading Czech sculptor Josef Myslbek. One of these depicts Ctirad and Šárka, two characters from Slavic mythology who feature in the Bohemian tale of *The Maiden's War*, in which women rise up against their male oppressors.

ROTUNDA OF ST MARTIN

K Rotundě, Vyšehrad

The rotunda is the only preserved medieval building in Vyšehrad and probably dates from the late eleventh century. It has subsequently functioned as both an ecclesiastical and a secular building. Initially it functioned as a church, possibly one belonging to Vyšehrad Castle until the Hussite Wars in the fifteenth century, when it was used variously as a small prison and a gunpowder storehouse. On one side of the rotunda, a cannonball is embedded in the wall as a result of the eighteenth-century Prussian attack.

LEOPOLD GATE

Vyšehrad

After the Thirty Years War had ended in 1648, the Habsburgs rebuilt the Vyšehrad complex in the Baroque style prevalent at the time, as part of a Catholic Counter-Reformation and to demonstrate the imperial power of the dynasty. The complex, which was used as a training centre for the imperial army, had two gateways, the Tábor and the more impressive Leopold with its three arches, one for traffic and the other two for pedestrians. Originally the gateway had a mechanized drawbridge and it is still possible to see remnants of it today.

OPEN-AIR THEATRE

Letní Scéna, Vyšehrad

Once a week during the summer months it is possible to see a musical performance of one type or another at this open-air theatre. It was established in the 1990s and was formerly a walled redan, one of five within the fortifications, built in 1850 and specifically aimed at the New Town in case of civil unrest. The theatre has performances as diverse as Shakespeare's *Romeo and Juliet* and the Lacus Mortis Festival, an annual event of singing, poetry recitals and other performances.

KOVAROVIC VILLA

Libušina, Vyšehrad

Josef Chochol (1880–1956), a Czech architect, was inspired by the Cubist works of Picasso and Braque to create this small, unusual villa in 1913. The clever use of the various planes and the angled window recesses allow natural light to reflect in different ways and create interesting shadows at different times of the day. To complement the house, the façade also utilizes Cubist ideas of form, including the gardens and even the wrought iron fencing around the property. The villa is one of several built by Chochol in the Cubist style.

LIBUŠE AND PŘEMYSL STATUE

Vyšehrad

One of the four statue groups in Vyšehrad Park by Josef Václav Myslbek is *Libuše and Přemysl*, the legendary ancestors of the Přemyslid dynasty of royals in the ninth century. According to legend, Libuše was a queen who had succeeded her father as ruler, and later married the ploughman Přemysl with whom she was in love. Legend also tells that Libuše foretold the greatness of Prague, declaring that she had a vision in which she saw 'A great city whose glory will touch the stars'.

NATIONAL LIBRARY OF TECHNOLOGY PRAGUE

Technická, Dejvice

The Dejvice district is traditionally a well-heeled residential area, but it is also home to university campuses and the National Library of Technology. The original library was situated in the Clementinum within the Old Town district but was relocated in 2009 when this purpose-built development was opened. The focal point of the interior is the series of 200 comic strip drawings by the Romanian artist Dan Perjovschi (b. 1961) in the atrium and stairwells. Although the library is fundamentally for the use of students, there are also a number of cultural events held here for the general public.

AIRSHIP ON THE ROOF OF DOX CENTRE FOR CONTEMPORARY ART

Poupětova, Holešovice

At the beginning of the twentieth century a series of industrial buildings were erected on this site, which continued to function as such for the next century. In 2002 the buildings were purchased by Leoš Válka (b. 1953), a Czech national who had returned from exile in Australia as a wealthy entrepreneur. Along with a team of partners, he transformed the buildings into the DOX Centre for Contemporary Arts, symbolic of the urban regeneration of the Holešovice District. The Gulliver Airship was erected in 2013, a reminder of human aspirations at the beginning of the twentieth century.

TROJA BRIDGE

Vltava River, Troja

The latest crossing of the Vltava is the Troja bowstring arch road bridge that links the districts of Holešovice and Troja just north of the city centre. The British structural engineering firm of Mott MacDonald, in partnership with the Czech architect Roman Koucký (b. 1959), designed the structure and it was opened in 2014. The bridge's span is 200 m (656 ft) and its overall length is 260 m (853 ft). The height of the arch is only 20 m (66 ft), making it one of the lowest of its type in the world.

DŽBÁN OUTDOOR SWIMMING LAKE

Divoká Šárka Nature Reserve

To the north-west of the central city of Prague is the Divoká Šárka Nature Reserve. Its name comes from a Czech legend about the female warrior Šárka who, during the Maiden's War, beguiled and entrapped the most powerful warrior of her enemies and then killed him. She then threw herself off the cliffs into the gorge at this location as an act of atonement for the betrayal. As well as the huge lake there is also a public swimming pool which is continuously fed by fresh water from the streams within the reserve.

JAPANESE GARDEN

Botanical Gardens, Troja

In the southern part of the Botanical Gardens is the Japanese Garden, an area of tranquillity with superb examples of Acers, although the emphasis is on evergreen planting. The Japanese Garden is one of several themed areas planned in this 49 ha (120 ac) site. The Botanical Gardens were established in 1968 and it was only in 1992 that they were accessible to the public. One of the main attractions is the 130 m (427 ft) long greenhouse Fata Morgana, opened in 2004, for the display of tropical species.

TROJA PALACE

U Trojského Zámku, Troja

A magnificent summer palace built in the seventeenth century for the Sternbergs, a leading aristocratic family, the building is now used as an exhibition space for nineteenth-century Czech art. The palace was the work of the French architect Jean Baptiste Mathey (1630–96), who defied the pervading taste for the Baroque in Prague in favour of a more Palladian style. The exception is the elaborate external staircase, which is distinctly Baroque. Mathey also designed the French–Italianate gardens that appear to have been inspired by those at Versailles, albeit on a much smaller scale.

VINEYARD OF ST KLÁRA

Troja

The tiny Baroque church of St Klára is at the highest point of the Troja district, and on the slopes below are its considerably older vineyards. Today the vineyard is part of the much larger Botanical Gardens of Prague and visitors can enjoy a wine trail to see both the varieties of grapes grown here and also their processing. The Vintners House has an exhibition of wine-making in the region and it is possible to sample some of its produce. A successful local white wine is *Bílé z Botanické*, a Riesling.

HVĚZDA SUMMER PALACE

Obora Hvězda Park

Hvězda means 'star' and this building takes its name from the unusual hexagram shape of the summer palace erected here in the mid-sixteenth century. Archduke Ferdinand of Tyrol (1529–95), a younger son of the King Ferdinand of Bohemia, commissioned the building, demonstrating his philosophical knowledge and symbolism of the hexagram, which was being used by both the Orthodox Catholic Church as well as by alchemists and followers of the occult. After the death of his father in 1564, Ferdinand took charge of the Tyrol, a region of Austria where he lived until his death.